"The funniest, toughest-minded, and most ingenious political satire I've read in years is Barbara Garson's *MacBird*. A veteran of the Berkeley student wars, Miss Garson has had the excellent and obvious notion—obvious after she did it—of savaging our political Establishment with a burlesque *Macbeth*. . . . It works surprisingly well, whether as sharply pointed satire or as sheer—or if you prefer, mere—high-spirited low-comedy fooling around; most commonly, as a peculiar mixture of both. That Shakespeare is Universal is well known, but, to Garsonize Lady Macbeth: Who would have thought the old bard had so much blood in him? . . .

"The most disturbing and 'controversial' aspect of *MacBird* is that the eponymous villain murders John Ken O'Dunc just as Macbeth murders Duncan. If this is taken to be the author's serious—or even satirical—implication, then her play sinks to the level of such ultra-rightist tracts as *A Texan Looks at Lyndon Johnson* or the post-assassination lucubrations of the palindromic professor, Dr. Revilo P. Oliver, and it would not be worth reading, let alone reviewing. But I don't so take it, for several reasons. An author who would build a satire around such an insinuation, for which no shred of evidence exists save in the addled wits of crackbrains, couldn't possibly have written anything as funny as *MacBird*, humor being incompatible with solipsistic fanaticism. Nor would such a writer be endowed with the sense of reality Miss Garson shows in her adaptation of the Shakespearean material, the joke always depending on deftly using the familiar old lines to comment on the actual current situation. The most obvious explanation seems also the best: That, having picked *Macbeth* as the Shakespearean play that best lent itself to topical satire, she was stuck with the plot line and, while she could (and did) make some changes, the central dramatic action, Macbeth's murder of Duncan, couldn't have been omitted without its becoming another play. . . .

"Although I am no friend of broad comedy, I find broadness here, given this particular subject, exhilarating and somehow liberating. So much dignified cant has overlaid the reality of our current Establishment politics that it is refreshing to have it brushed aside by a ruthless, if over-exuberant, housekeeper. . . . And she has solved, in her own slam-bang way, the problem of satirizing a reality so grotesque that it often seems to defy exaggeration, producing its own built-in parody, so to speak. . . .

"At last the younger generation has produced a satirist."

—Dwight Macdonald,
The New York Review of Books

"Certainly, the most explosive play thus far turned up by the third theater is Barbara Garson's *MacBird*. . . . This work immediately establishes its young author as an extraordinary gifted parodist, for in converting *Macbeth* to her own uses, she demonstrates an unusual ear for Shakespearean verse and an impressive ability to adapt the rhythms and accents of a past age to a modern idiom. . . .

"The seditious implications of *MacBird* are clear and apparent—it is a work in which all political leaders are seen as calculating, power-hungry and bloody, and nobody comes off well. But although the play is bound to start a storm of protest (not all of it unjustified) and may even be suppressed by some government agency, it will very probably go down as one of the brutally provocative works in the American theater, as well as one of the most grimly amusing."

—Robert Brustein, *The New York Times*

"The run on *MacBird* . . . is based largely on its arch and outrageous proposition that the so-called Kennedy-Johnson rivalry has parallels in Shakespeare's classic tragedy about the lust for power. Mrs. Garson exploits these possibilities with clever irony, casting Lyndon Johnson in the Macbeth role, John F. Kennedy as the Duncan figure and Robert Kennedy as a combination Malcolm-Macduff.

"Mrs. Garson uses a gift for rapier-like caricature to demolish most of America's political leadership."

—Leroy F. Aarons, *The Washington Post*

"The terror of this work, already gathering a reputation in underground literature, is profound. But *MacBird,* however irresponsible, seditious and shocking it might be, is simply an intensification of many dark fears and suspicions that are now coming to light. As such, it is only a sign of the general malaise eating away at the nation today, and there, at heart, is the real terror for us all."

—Richard Christiansen, *Chicago Daily News*

"Up from the underground comes this shocking parody of *Macbeth*—shocking because America has known little of vicious satire. Tom Lehrer's songs and the popular night club 'black humorists' have never dared with this young woman has done. . . .

"No punches are pulled back from the Macbeth story. There are touches of Hamlet and Julius Caesar, also, chiefly to electrify us by considering famous speeches in terms of today."

—Thorpe Menn, *The Kansas City Star*

"America's under-30 generation has already spawned a poet named Dylan, a novelist named Pynchon, and a prophet named Savio. And now it has found its playwright in 26-year-old Barbara Garson, whose parody-play *MacBird* is of Swiftian dimension. . . .

"But the real power of *MacBird* rests not on its ability to capture in satire Lyndon Johnson's private character, but on its writing. Miss Garson has an uncanny ear for the cadences and rhythms of Shakespeare."

—Jack Newfield, *The Village Voice*

"Let me make something absolutely clear. I do not believe in censorship. I don't want it, and I wouldn't support it. I do not question the right of this young lady to publish, sell or shout her literary works, and I support her in that right. I have no criticism for those who buy and enjoy her work. That is a private matter, involving the free choice of seller and buyer, and so be it."

—Barry Goldwater, *The Los Angeles Times*

MACBIRD!

BY BARBARA GARSON

GROVE PRESS, INC.   NEW YORK

FOREWORD

MacBird originated in August, 1965, as a slip
of the tongue when Barbara Garson, speaking at
an anti-war rally in Berkeley, California, quite ac-
cidentally referred to the First Lady of the United
States as Lady MacBird Johnson. Since it was just
a few weeks after the Watts insurrection and the
Berkeley troop-train demonstrations, the opening
lines of a play suggested themselves immediately:
"When shall we three meet again/In riot, strike,
or stopping train?"

She decided to write a fifteen-minute skit or
playlet based on *MacBeth* to be performed at the
October 15-16 International Days of Protest. By
October 15 there was no skit, however, for she was
embarked upon a full-length play.

In December she took a completed first-draft
manuscript with her on a trip to New York and
showed it to Roy Levine, an old friend with experience in the theater as a stage designer. He and
Julia Curtis, then working as a secretary at Ran-
dom House, decided on the spot that the play
could and should be performed professionally in
New York. Barbara was skeptical, but told them
they were free to try. Within a year, by Christmas
of 1966, a professional production had been fully
capitalized and cast and was in rehearsal, with Julia
producing and Roy directing.

During the Spring of 1966 the entire first draft was printed by the Independent Socialist Club of Berkeley, in an edition of 2,000 copies which sold out in six weeks; extensive excerpts appeared in the Berkeley magazine *Despite Everything*; but otherwise *MacBird* was known only by the New York literati among whom Julia Curtis had been circulating manuscripts.

By August, 1966, the play had been read and warmly praised by such important literary figures as Robert Lowell, Eric Bentley, and Robert Brustein, but still no major magazine or publisher was willing to touch it. The author's husband, Marvin Garson, decided to publish the play himself, establishing for that purpose the Grassy Knoll Press. Five thousand copies of *MacBird* were printed at the Berkeley Free Press, an all-night leaflet factory which the Garsons had helped establish during the Free Speech Movement in 1964. The first printing disappeared in a few weeks. By January the Grassy Knoll had turned green, having gone through five printings totaling 105,000 copies.

Meanwhile, events off-stage followed the script. The conflict between Lyndon Johnson and Robert Kennedy, barely in evidence a year before, had broken out into the open. The Warren Report, so recently a sacred text, was now widely considered as an attempt to reassure the nation rather than to enlighten it. The President's prestige had fallen so low that what had been prophecy now read as a statement of current political fact: "He's so de-

spised it's fash'nable in fact/To call him villain,
tweak him by the nose,/ Break with his party and
jeer him in the press."

* * *

The text as it now stands is almost half again
as long as the first-draft manuscript of December,
1965. The author wrote many new lines and several new scenes in the Spring of 1966, working in
close consultation with Roy Levine to make the
play more unified dramatically. This new material
appeared in the Grassy Knoll Press edition and will
appear in the Penguin edition to be published
shortly in Britain. Some of it appeared in the ver-
sion of *MacBird* carried in *City Lights Journal #3*.
The extensive excerpts printed in *Ramparts* magazine followed the text of the first draft. The present
Grove Press edition contains all the material from
the Grassy Knoll Press edition plus many of the
changes and additions made during the first two
weeks of rehearsals.

MacBird was first presented at the Village Gate theater in New York on January 19, 1967. It was produced by Julia Curtis and David Dretzin and directed by Roy Levine. The original cast, in order of appearance, was:

Prologue	Dalton Dearborn
1st Witch	Jennifer Darling
2nd Witch	Cleavon Little
3rd Witch	Tony Capodilupo
John Ken O'Dunc	Paul Hecht
Robert Ken O'Dunc	William Devane
Ted Ken O'Dunc	John Pleshette
MacBird	Stacy Keach
Crony	David Spielberg
Aide	Joel Zwick
Lady MacBird	Rue McClanahan
Earl of Warren	John Clark
Egg of Head	Dalton Dearborn
Reporters	Cleavon Little and Paul Hecht
First Daughter	Deborah Gordon
Second Daughter	Jennifer Darling
Wayne of Morse	Paul Hecht
Messenger	Deborah Gordon

Senators, Congressmen, Aides, Spectators, etc.

PROLOGUE

Enter middle-aged man dressed in standard business attire except for a plume in his hat and a toy sword at his waist.

Oh, for a fireless muse, that could descend
From kingdoms, princes, monarchs, and the like
To common themes of marital affairs,
Of young romance and adolescent strife;
Then should our warlike leaders not appear
Upon this stage in false resemblances
Twixt princes of the present and the past.
Oh, pardon, gentles, these bright-painted spirits,
That, drawn too clear, seem more than what they
    say.
Can costumed kings who sweep across this stage
With antique garb and flashing swords of old
Be likened to our sober-suited leaders,
Who plot in prose their laceless, graceless deeds?
And think you that within these wooden walls
Can be confined two warring dynasties,
With swelling hosts of hacks, and clerks, and claques
Whose high uprearèd and abutting prides
Now rip a ruling monolith asunder?
Can these bare boards support the vast machines
That now sustain two modern monarchies?
No, this weak wood but holds the airy actors
Who here portray fantastic lords of yore.

1

Oh, don't employ your own imaginations
To piece out imperfections in our plot.
For things that seem, I beg you, know no seeming;
Your very lack of thoughts must cloak our kings.
For my sake, seek no silly suppositions;
Disdain to note what likenesses may show;
Accept our words, ignore your intuitions;
For *honi soit qui mal y pense*, you know.

ACT ONE

SCENE ONE

Hotel corridor at Democratic convention. THREE
WITCHES *slink in. The* 1ST WITCH *is dressed as a
student demonstrator, beatnik stereotype. The* 2ND
WITCH *is a Negro with the impeccable grooming
and attire of a* Muhammad Speaks *salesman. The*
3RD WITCH *is an old leftist, wearing a worker's cap
and overalls. He carries a lunch pail and a lantern.*

1ST WITCH:
> When shall we three meet again?

2ND WITCH:
> In riot!

3RD WITCH:
> > Strike!

1ST WITCH:
> > Or stopping train?

2ND WITCH:
> When the hurly-burly's done,
> When the race is lost or won.

3RD WITCH:
> Out on the convention floor.
> Or in some hotel corridor.

3

1ST WITCH:

> Where cheering throngs can still be heard,
> There to meet with . . . MacBird!

A cry off-stage.

2ND WITCH:

> I come, soul brothers!

3RD WITCH:

> Comrades call!

1ST WITCH:

> Away!

WITCHES *move off, chanting.*

THREE WITCHES:

> Fair is foul and foul is fair.
> Hover through stale and smoke-filled air.

*Hotel room at Democratic Convention. The walls
are covered with charts and maps showing current
tally of votes, areas of strength, etc. In an armchair
at one corner sits* TED *playing solitaire.* JOHN *and*
ROBERT *enter. They move and look alike, except
that* JOHN *is bigger and more self-assured.*

JOHN:
> Like? Dislike? What foolishness is that?
> Our cause demands suppressing sentiment.

ROBERT:
> But, Jack, you know it isn't merely scruples.
> He has a fat, yet hungry look. Such men are
> dangerous.

JOHN:
> Good God, this womanly whimpering just
> when I need your manly immorality!

ROBERT:
> But John—but Jack—you know it isn't that—

JOHN:
> Enough is said! At least we have to ask.
> He won't accept and, even if he does,
> His name will just stand second on the ticket.
> You, Bob, are still the second in succession.

And Ted is next ... and princes yet unborn ...
And for this land, this crownèd continent,
This earth of majesty, this seat of Mars,
This forceful breed of men, this mighty world,
I see a ... *New Frontier* beyond her seas.
She shall o'erflow her shores and burst her
    banks,
Eastward extend till East does meet with West,
And West until the West does touch the East
And o'er this hot and plaguèd earth descend
The Pox Americana, a sweet haze,
Shelt'ring all the world in its deep shade.
And our descendants, locking link to link,
Shall lay a lofty line of lovèd kings
To serve the faithful, laying low the foe;
Guiding, guarding, governing this folk.

TED:

Gee, that's keen! (*Counting on his fingers.*)
So let's see ... That means Jack in '60 and '64,
then Bobby in '68 and '72, then me in ... what
would that make it ... '76 and '80 and then in
1984 it could be ...

ROBERT:

Shut up, Teddy! Can't you see we're busy?

JOHN:

There's much that must be seen and done and
    heard.
Let's first bestow the title on Macbird.

Exit JOHN, ROBERT *and* TED. *Enter* WITCHES.

3RD WITCH:
Where have *you* been, brother?

2ND WITCH:
In L. A.

1ST WITCH:
How's the weather there?

2ND WITCH:
It's wondrous warm,
And all the world's abroad, out laughin',
boppin'.
A joyful throng comes pouring out of doors
A brick in either hand—they're goin' shoppin'.
O blessèd, blessèd blaze, the land's alight!
And I have never seen so sweet a sight.

3RD WITCH:
And sister, where were you?

1ST WITCH:
A troop train taking men to Viet Land
Came chugging, chugging, chugging through
our town.
"Halt ho!" quoth I, and stood upon the track,
Then, tossing leaflets, leaped up to the troops:
"Turn back, turn back and stop this train.
Why fight for them and die in vain?"
But we were few and so did fail:
Shoved off the train, we went to jail.
Yet trouble stirred is always for the good.

3RD WITCH:
>Quite right, young witch. Constant agitation
>Has been assigned as our historic task.
>Some precepts from the past, herein entombed
>   ... (*Lifts lantern.*)

2ND WITCH:
>That same old torch ...

3RD WITCH:
>   At least it casts some light.
>Young witch, it's time you learned these lasting
>   lessons.
>Be thou militant but by no means adventurist.
>The working class and their objective interests
>Grapple to our cause with hoops of steel.
>But never water down the party's program
>For petty bourgeois students and the like.
>Neither a burrower from within nor a leader
>   be,
>But stone by stone construct a conscious cadre.
>And this above all—to thine own class be true
>And it must follow, as the very next depression,
>Thou canst not then be false to revolution.

2ND WITCH:
>Yeah, pops, yeah.

1ST WITCH:
>   We really understand.

3RD WITCH:
>Tell us more about L.A.

Loud footsteps, door slams off-stage.

1ST WITCH (*whisper*):

> Who's there?

2ND WITCH:
> Here comes MacBird. Quick! Hide behind the
> chair.

The WITCHES *scurry away, concealing themselves insufficiently. In the meantime* MAC BIRD
*enters, a large heavy-jowled figure, followed by
his* CRONY, *a thin sharpy.*

MAC BIRD:
> So foul, unfair a day I've never seen.
> (*He notes figures behind the chair.*)
> Some delegates, I guess, or shy supporters.
> (*Toward chair:*) Why howdy there!
> (*To* CRONY:) Let's give them folks a thrill.
> The name's MacBird! I'm mighty proud to
> meet ya!

Extends hand toward chair. WITCHES *rise up
slowly from behind.*

> Why, it's a nigra and a filthy beatnik.

CRONY:
> And there's a bum done up in worker's duds.

MAC BIRD:
> God damn! Those beatnik picketers all over!

CRONY:

    Perhaps I better run and call the cops.

MAC BIRD:

    Now just calm down. I know how to deal with
        people.
    I'll handle this.
    (*To* WITCHES:) OK, let's hear your story.

WITCHES *move eerily out from behind chair.*

    Come on, speak up, now what in thunder are
        you?

1ST WITCH:

    All hail MacBird! All hail the Senate's leader!

2ND WITCH:

    All hail MacBird, Vice-President thou art!

3RD WITCH:

    All hail MacBird, that shall be President!

ALL WITCHES:

    All hail MacBird, that shall be President!

CRONY:

    Hey boss, how come you gulp and seem to fear?
    It has a kind of pretty sound I think.
    (*To* WITCHES:) If you can look into your crystal
        ball
    And say who'll get ahead and who'll go down,
    Speak then to me. When he becomes the chief
    What will I be?

1ST WITCH:

> You'll be his leading hack.

2ND WITCH:

> It's not so high, but so much less to fall;
> For you shall share the fate of his career.
> MacBird shall be the mightiest of all,
> But Ken O'Dunc alone shall leave an heir.

3RD WITCH:

> An heir who'll play a king, like other kings.
> He too shall be an extra on our set.
> He'll strut and fret his hour on the boards
> And be applauded wildly from the pit.
> But if you skip and read a later page,
> *We* take the final bow upon this stage.

MAC BIRD (*who has been absorbed in his thoughts*):

> The Senate leader, that I *know* I am.
> But how Vice-President, when Ken O'Dunc
> Despises me like dirt? And to be chief—
> Unthinkable while Ken O'Dunc holds sway!

WITCHES *start to slither off the stage.*

> Stay, you lying varmints! Tell me more!
> Where'd you learn this hogwash that you tell?
> And why the devil did you come to me?
> Come on! Speak out!

CRONY:

> They're gliding off the stage.

WITCHES (*continuing to move off, and chanting together*):

The bosses shall be booted in the bin,
The kings unkinged. We have a world to win!

MAC BIRD:
Vice-President—and President to be!

CRONY:
It's not the *natural* path to reach the top.

Enter BOBBY.

ROBERT:
Hail MacBird, Vice-President thou art—
That is, if you'll accept the second place.
My brother Jack has picked you for the job
And hopes that you'll agree to grace his slate.

MAC BIRD (*aside*):
Vice-President—and President to be!

ROBERT:
I know of course it's not what you had hoped.
It's really just an honorary post.
And so I'm sure you must want time to think.
Perhaps we'll get together late tonight.

MAC BIRD:
I thank your brother. Let him know for me
I do accept with deep humility.

ROBERT (*faltering*):
Well . . . That's just fine . . . I guess that means
    that we . . .
Should go and meet together some time . . .
    soon.

MAC BIRD (*firmly*):
We've got a lot to do. Today. But when?

ROBERT:
At ten o'clock?

MAC BIRD:
OK, I'll see you then.

Scene Three

Ken O'Dunc's hotel room. On stage are JOHN *and* ROBERT *surrounded by a group of their advisors. In a chair in the corner sits* TED.

ROBERT (*gossiping with circle*):
   And just like that, he took it on the spot.

   Group gasps, showing surprise and dismay.

JOHN:
   Unity required that we ask him.

ROBERT:
   The party must be made to speak as one.

JOHN:
   Consensus, lords, consensus is the thing!

ROBERT:
   The jewel upon the crown that marks the king.

JOHN:
   So gentlemen, that's now the way it stands.

   Enter MAC BIRD. *Conversation stops short but* MAC BIRD *proceeds heartily.*

MAC BIRD:
   Howdy, folks. (*Pause with no response.*)

14

I want to thank you all. (*Earnestly*.)
I know you all conferred in choosing me.
I wonder if you know just what this means
To me, a boy who nearly dropped from school?
Vice-President of these United States!
Why, it's an inspiration to *all* boys
Who daily toil, and sometimes feel despair,
To know that in the White House—or quite
    near—
There dwells a man who had to work like them,
Who knew the struggles, knew the ups and
    downs.
It gives a boy a faith in this, our land.

JOHN:

And we in turn thank *you,* your quick
    response.

MAC BIRD:

Why thanks.

JOHN:

Thank *you.* (*More formally*.)
           Friends, brothers, lords,
All you who are nearest to us, know
We will establish our estate upon
The eldest, Robert, whom we now do name
The Lord of Laws, henceforth our closest
    counsel.
In all affairs of state we are as one.
To him entrust your thoughts as though to me.
And now to plan the tone of our campaign.

> (*Turning to an aide*:) Have you the calculations
>   I requested?

AIDE:

> Aye, here my liege, the output's based upon
> A partial computation of the data.

> AIDE *holds out IBM output sheets to* JOHN, *but*
> MAC BIRD *gets hold of them.*

MAC BIRD:

> A powerful mess o' numbers. Pray, what's that?

AIDE:

> A psychosexual index of the symbols
> We use in predetermining his image
> With variables projected . . . if you please!
> (*At "if you please" he takes it rudely from* MAC-
> BIRD *and gives it to* JOHN.)
> The final print-out can't be made till morning.

JOHN:

> These findings, sir, we shall peruse withal.

> JOHN, ROBERT *and* FOLLOWERS *go over to desk*
> *where they are poring over the figures.*

MAC BIRD:

> Why stay we now? What use is here for me?

CRONY:

> Dare they presume to scorn you in this man-
>   ner?

MAC BIRD:

> With forty years campaigning 'neath my belt,
> They turn from me to mind a damn machine.

CRONY:

If they could come to know your worship's
worth . . .

MAC BIRD:

And did you hear that snippet! . . . "if you
please"?

CRONY:

I heard. I said not much, yet think the more.

MAC BIRD:

I am a sorry second in this slate.

CRONY:

Up here you're disadvantaged in their sight.
A very sorry second, as you say.
But yon, you are the pinnacle of power;
What vast domains where you are best beloved!
Were it not wise to bring them to your
        kingdom
By such invention as we can devise
So they can feel the force of your supporters,
Hear it, sense it, see it with their eyes?

MAC BIRD:

Aye, there'll be some to stand up for me there.
(*To* JOHN:) Say, how about conferring on my
ranch?

ROBERT:

We're all engaged until the coronation.

MAC BIRD:

And after that?

ROBERT:
>Why then we'll have to see.

MAC BIRD:
>The wife and I would gladly organize
>A welcome worthy of our honored guest.
>We'll have a grand procession through the
>>streets
>For you to greet the people of my state.

JOHN:
>When all the coronation plans are through,
>We'll surely visit then.

ROBERT:
>>For now, adieu.

JOHN:
>Adieu, MacBird. We'll see you by the by.

ROBERT:
>Adieu.

MAC BIRD:
>Adieu my lords, adieu.

Exit all except MAC BIRD.

This Lord of Laws be blasted, there's the rub
For in my way it lies. Stars, hide thy fires.
Let no light see my black and deep desires.

A room on the MacBird ranch. LADY MAC BIRD *is seated at her desk and reading aloud from a letter.*

LADY MAC BIRD:

". . . and these weird critters had no sooner slithered out when in strides Bobby, the punky younger brother, trumpeting out their very words. 'Hail MacBird, Vice-President thou art.' I don't know what the devil they are but I reckon it's something mighty deep. So now it's two down and one to go. I'll be home straight from here and we can puzzle out these strange happenings together. I just wanted you to know right away, my dearest little pardner, what we have and what's been promised. Be seeing you real soon,

Your loving Bird."

(*Putting letter aside.*)

All hail MacBird, the President to be!
And yet I fear you're not direct enough.
The naked act would scandalize your eye.
You need to dress it up, to drape it out,
In purple prose that robes it nobly.
Your mind's too full of all your own conceits
To catch the nearest way, the clearest way.

You're not without ambition, but you lack
The forthrightness to face your own desire.
You'd take the gold and never ask the source.
You'd swindle if the act were vague enough
And yet you'd never swipe it clean and clear,
For lack of means to mystify the deed.
How often in the past have I arranged
To have the right connections come your way,
Myself performing all the devious acts
So you receive the bounty graciously.
How artfully you've learned to look away
While I prepare the props and set the stage.
Then enter thou, declaiming loftily,
Forgetting the deceit that makes for art.
There's much you wish were done but would
    not do
For fear you'd see too clear your own intent.
What you want highly you want holily . . .

MAC BIRD *enters.*

All hail MacBird!

MAC BIRD:
        All hail, sweet innocent!

LADY MAC BIRD:
All hail MacBird, the President to be!
Your letters have transported me beyond
This feeble present and I feel the surge
Of future power now.

MAC BIRD:
           My dearest bird,

To your nest of tasty tidings add this news.
Short upon the royal coronation,
The king intends to visit our domain.

LADY MAC BIRD (*aside*):
Then fate doth mean to have thee crowned,
it seems.

MAC BIRD:
My plan is to impress them with my power.
Not only will I show them round the ranch
But I'll expose them to our faithful followers.

LADY MAC BIRD:
Expose him to the fury of his foes.

MAC BIRD:
Expose him?

LADY MAC BIRD:

Just expose him. Nothing more.
I mean but what you meant, but what you
want.
Your broad dominions shelter not a few
Who'd show great force of feeling for their
chief.

MAC BIRD:

I dare do all that may become a man.
Who dares do more is none.

LADY MAC BIRD:

I'm not a man.
I am a lady and a Southern hostess.
With simple signs of hospitality
I mean to give our guests the warmest welcome.

MAC BIRD:

We shall discuss it further.

LADY MAC BIRD:

He that's coming
Must be provided for, and you shall put
The day's great business into my dispatch
Which shall to all our days and nights to come
Give solely sovereign sway and masterdom.

A coronation scene. Ken O'Dunc's procession mounts to podium amidst regal splendor. MAC BIRD *and* CRONY *are at the end of the dais on which* KEN O'DUNC *is standing flanked by dignitaries. The* EARL OF WARREN, *carrying the crown, stands next to* KEN O'DUNC. *The "Hallelujah Chorus" plays in the background as he speaks.*

EARL:

    It is my office to set this sacred symbol
    Upon the realm's elect anointed head.
    I have, and will, for past and coming kings
    Thus handed up to each the reins of state.
    But never have I felt as here today,
    That sov'reignty rests not in crown or sceptre
    But in the very person of this prince.
    Never was monarch better feared or loved
    Than this majesty. There's nowhere found a
        subject
    That nods not in fair consent and loyalty;
    There's not, I think a subject in the realm
    That sits in anger or uneasiness
    Under the sweet shade of thy government.
    Oh, thou shalt bring us blessed peace and
        plenty,
    But also bring a brilliance never dulled.

For ever and ever thy greater glory ring,
And I shall toll thy tale, yea, true and clear.
O lord of lords, forever reign renowned!
O world, rejoice! A king of kings is crowned!

"Hallelujah Chorus" swells. EARL OF WARREN
*places crown on Ken O'Dunc's head. Much
cheering, which dies down as* KEN O'DUNC
begins to speak.

JOHN (*voice over loudspeaker, echoing*):
We celebrate in this uplifting hour
A vict'ry not for person, nor for party,
But a promise of renewal for the realm.
For I have sworn before almighty God,
The potency and power of my youth
Shall not be stinted but shall freely flow
Upon our broad and ever fertile fields.

MAC BIRD (*downstage*):
It's a cold day in January.

CRONY:

Yeah.

JOHN:
To those who think our greater glories gone,
Who think that we have softened as we aged,
I warn that you will find us fully ripe;
Ripe in riches, ripe in readiness.
This century will find us ripe to rule!
Let every nation know, both weak and mighty
That we'll pay any price, bear any burden,

Meet any hardship, challenge any foe
To strengthen, to secure and spread our system.
And though our strength be vast and over-
  powering
(For dare we ever tempt the foe with weakness?)
We shall not force small nations to their knees.
We never shall, as tyrants, tie them to us;
Our force shall only force them to be free.
Yea, we must be a giant generation,
Geared for glory, seared in sacrifice.
Ask not how you can profit off your country,
But ask what you can give to serve the state.
Ask not how you can make your family prosper,
But ask how you can make your nation great.

*The music of "Pomp and Circumstance" rises
in the background.*

Wider still and wider grow our bound'rics.

MAC BIRD:

It's still damn cold but now it's getting clear.

JOHN:

The question each must ask and each must
  answer
Is: "How can I help reach that new frontier?"

MAC BIRD:

This here is the winter of our discontent,
Made odious by that son of . . .

CRONY:

                    Yeah.

MAC BIRD:

    Now do our princelings pipe in tenor tones,
    Our bass-voiced elder statesmen cast aside,
    Our ancient counselors yield to college pups;
    Grim-visaged politics has smoothed his face;
    Our manly wars give way to mincing words;
    And now instead of mounting saddled steeds,
    To fright the souls of fearful adversaries,
    He capers nimbly at a yachting party,
    He struts before the wanton ambling nymph.
    But I am not cut out for merry meetings,
    For fancy foods and poetry and lutes.
    I am stamped out in stern and solid shape,
    And thank the lord I lack the frippery
    To sport and blithely laugh in foreign tongues
    While lightly touching on affairs of state
    At fox hunts, polo parties, garden teas.
    Yes, I am made of sturdy, homespun stuff.
    My friends and foes alike know where I stand.
    I do not lisp in light and lacy lies.

JOHN:

    MacBird!

MAC BIRD:

        My friend! I'm proud to shake your hand!

JOHN:

    Thanks. You and I must get together shortly;
    Your duties need defining, carefully.

MAC BIRD:

    Well, how about that meeting on my ranch?

JOHN:

I have some business here a day or two.

MAC BIRD:

Then come next week. 'Twill give us time to
plan.
My wife and I intend a bang-up show.
We'll hold a grand procession through the
streets
So you can meet the people of my state.
You'll ride in rich regalia through the throng,
And feel the warmth and frenzy of their love.

JOHN:

That's fine, MacBird. We'll see you in a week.
Adieu, MacBird.

MAC BIRD:

Adieu, y'all.

ALL:

Adieu.

Exit all except MAC BIRD.

MAC BIRD:

I dare not think the thought. But let that be
Which the eye fears, when the hand has done,
to see.

SCENE SIX

The MacBird ranch. MAC BIRD *in dressing gown.*

LADY MAC BIRD:
>The guest rooms are ready. The feast is all
>   prepared.

MAC BIRD:
>I hope the entertainment's not too flashy.

LADY MAC BIRD:
>There's nothing which itself is in bad taste.
>The elegance of touch is all that counts.
>It's up to us.

MAC BIRD:
>   If we should fail?

LADY MAC BIRD:
>   We—fail?
>The only danger lies in faltering.
>The boldest deed, the biggest lie wins out.
>This lesson we have learned from Ken O'Dunc.
>Remember he attacked that rebel isle,
>Denied he did it, then announced: "Twas I"?
>The major thing is confidence and style,
>For still the world believes he'd never lie.

MAC BIRD:

Indeed the man's a dangerous hypocrite.
This nation needs old-fashioned honesty.
It needs a man with moral might and will;
It needs a man of deep sincerity.

Noise of motor.

LADY MAC BIRD:

Hark, hark! His helicopter o'er the range!

MAC BIRD:

You greet our fork-tongued guest, while I go
change.

Noise of helicopter landing. Exit MAC BIRD.
Enter JOHN *with* ROBERT, TEDDY *and entourage.*

ROBERT:

That it is, an oil well in the garden.

TEDDY:

Bobby, look. There's moo-moos on the lawn.

1ST MAN:

Luncheons on the grass here must be charming.

2ND MAN:

I understand they roast the oxen whole.

JOHN (*seeing* LADY MAC BIRD *and calling aloud*):

Lady MacBird! Good day, our gentle hostess.
Your rustic homestead charms us.

LADY MAC BIRD:

Thank you'all

Although this welcome's humble, be assured
We're honored to receive you at the ranch.
And simple folk throughout this ample state
Are clamoring to see you. So for them,
This Friday noon we've planned a grand
    parade,
A fitting welcome, where the passionate throng
Will line the streets and fill the buildings
    round.
At doors and windows, yea, on chimney tops,
Their infants in their arms, like that they'll
    stand,
The live-long day with patient expectation
To see their leader pass the streets downtown.
And when they see your open carriage near,
They'll raise a din and universal shout.

JOHN:
    This welcome planned unduly honors us.

LADY MAC BIRD:
    I hope you'll stay till Friday.

JOHN:
                    Yes, that's fine.

LADY MAC BIRD:
    MacBird awaits within; let's go and dine.

All exit into ranch.

SCENE SEVEN

A downtown street. The backdrop is a line drawing showing a six-story building toward the left, a grassy hill and a railroad overpass toward the right. A crowd lines the street, standing at the front of the stage with their backs to the audience, so that the parade route is imagined to be between the crowd and the backdrop. Crowd may be represented by a few people, with sound effects taken from a baseball game or other grossly disproportionate roaring throng.

1ST VOICE:
    So rich!

2ND VOICE:
        So young!

3RD VOICE:
        And yet so wise and sure.

1ST VOICE:
    It feels so safe to know he's there.

4TH VOICE (*male*):
        Aw, hell!
    He's just a politician like the rest.

3RD VOICE:

Oh, hush, you fool. He's there protecting us.
He gives his youth and strength to keep us free.

1ST VOICE:

And still has time to help out with the kids.

2ND VOICE:

This morning's paper showed his little girl
Dressed up in Mommy's shoes. It's on page
three.

1ST VOICE:

I love those kids as if they were my own.

4TH VOICE:

You make me sick.

3RD VOICE:

Shut up, you grouch!

1ST VOICE:

What's that?

2ND VOICE:

His car just came in sight. You see it there?

*Heads turn left and follow the path of an
imagined vehicle across the stage.*

ALL (*chanting in unison*):

He's coming . . . he's coming . . . he's going . . .
he's going . . .

A shot rings out.

ONE VOICE:

> He's gone!

Right after the shot is heard, a projector throws an X in a sixth-floor window of the building, trajectory lines extend from the building to the sidewalk, lettering appears, reading "Grassy Knoll," "Railroad Overpass," etc. In this way the backdrop becomes a newspaper diagram of the assassination scene.

1ST VOICE:
Oh, no!

2ND VOICE:
> Can't be!

3RD VOICE:
> They've shot the President!

5TH VOICE:
Oh, piteous sight!

1ST VOICE:
> Oh, noble Ken O'Dunc!

2ND VOICE:
Oh, woeful scene!

6TH VOICE:
> Oh, traitorous villainy!

2ND VOICE:
They shot from there.

1ST VOICE:

No, that way.

3RD VOICE:

Did you see?

4TH VOICE:
Let's get the facts. Let's go and watch TV.

Crowd runs off the stage shouting.

CROWD:
C'mon, c'mon!
It's that way!
Yeah!
Let's go!

A COP *remains on the stage and takes a piece of paper out of his pocket.*

COP:
It says the shots will be from that way sent.
I'll get that skunk who killed our President!
(*Strides off toward building with determination.*)

Scene Eight

The public street. Crowd drifts back in. Among them LADY MAC BIRD *to one side;* TED *and* ROBERT *over to the other side, looking furtive; and the* COP *with a rifle in his hand.*

VOICE:

    The nation weeps as one. All work is stopped.
    The men desert the plants. The schools are
        shut.
    The housewife leaves her pots; the food is
        burnt.
    The cars and public buses quit their routes.
    All private cares forgotten, strangers stop
    And ask each other questions on the street.

1ST VOICE:

    What news?

2ND VOICE:

    I heard they've taken someone in.

LADY MAC BIRD (*to* COP):

    Is't known who did this more than bloody
        deed?

COP:

    He's a notorious traitor. Here, take this weapon

35

(*Hands it to someone.*)
Which I have just discovered on the spot.

1ST VOICE:
Why'd he do it?

3RD VOICE:
Has the cur denied it?

COP:
The wretch in part confessed his villainy.

LADY MAC BIRD:
Where is the viper? Bring the villain forth!

Enter MAC BIRD.

MAC BIRD (*striding to center of stage*):
That snake is dead who killed our President.

1ST VOICE:
What—dead?

2ND VOICE:
Who did it?

3RD VOICE:
Wherefore did he so?

MAC BIRD:
Who could refrain when Ken O'Dunc lies
dead?
Who could be calm that saw that scoundrel
grin?
Who could be loyal yet neutral? I tell thee, no
man.

ROBERT (*whispering to* TED):
>   What should be spoken here I dare not say.

TED:
>   What will you do? We are the rightful heirs.

ROBERT:
>   Keep still. The nearer in blood, the nearer
>   bloody.

TED:
>   There's something rotten in the State of—

VOICE:
>   Lady MacBird is fainting!

LADY MAC BIRD:
>   Oh, some air . . .
>   (*She falls to the ground. Great hubbub around
>   her.*)

1ST VOICE:
>   What's next?

3RD VOICE:
>   The world's gone mad!

4TH VOICE:
>   This country's doomed!

MAC BIRD (*stepping up on platform and addressing
   crowd in deliberate grand manner*):
>   Good countrymen, this madness must abate.
>   Be calm, my friends; I speak as head of state.

ACT TWO

SCENE ONE

A rotunda. A flag-draped coffin upstage, with mourners filing past. Enter ROBERT *and* TED.

TED:

> What should we do?

ROBERT:

> This murderous gun that's shot
> Is not yet empty, so our safest course
> Is to avoid its aim.

TED:

> Well then, let's flee.

ROBERT:

> You make a better target when you're
> bounding
> Through empty fields, a silhouetted form.
> I think it's safer milling in the herd
> Where any shot may hit another mark.
> The hunter must give pause when he observes
> A single shot may cause a wild stampede.

TED:

> Then you'll stay here?

ROBERT:

> At least until I know
> What forces may be brought against MacBird.

TED:

I'll go. You stay. Denounce him to the world.

ROBERT:

No good, not yet. Let's fight with subtle words
Till time lends friends and friends their
    trusted swords.

Exit TED.

A man, full man, I need to fight with me.

Enter EGG OF HEAD.

Lord Stevenson, the Egg of Head! How now?

EGG:

No feeble words of mine can hope to ease
This double grief, the nation's and your own.
Oh, what a noble mind was here brought
    down!
The statesman's, soldier's, scholar's eye, tongue,
    sword,
The expectancy and rose of this fair state,
The glass of fashion and the mold of form,
Supreme in war and thus our hope for peace,
The believed of all believers—quite, quite
    dead.
And I, of statesmen most deject and wretched,
That sucked the honey of his many vows,
Now see that noble and most sovereign leader
His silver skin laced with his own bright blood,
That unmatched form and feature of grown
    youth,

Blasted with a rifle. Woe is me!
To see what I have seen; see what I shall see!

ROBERT:

Again, Great Egg, your tongue gilds even death.
Your well-draped words oft veil a bloody fact.
(*Conspiratorially.*)
"To see what I have seen; see what I shall see."
Perhaps you share my fears of what's to come.
Perhaps you share my doubts on what was
    done.

EGG:

I've heard some talk, I've thought some
    thoughts, but I
Prefer to wait, to give MacBird a chance.
This new regime, though watered with warm
    blood,
May grow and bloom in peace. As to your
    doubts,
There's rumors round but I have seen no
    proof.

ROBERT:

There's proof enough for one who wants to see.

EGG:

To see, or not to see? That is the question.
Whether 'tis wiser as a statesman to ignore
The gross deception of outrageous liars,
Or to speak out against a reign of evil
And by so doing, end there for all time

The chance and hope to work within for change.

To work within the framework, there's the rub.

For who would bear the whips and scorns from boors,

The oppressor's wrongs, the proud man's contumely,

The insolence of office and the spurns

My patient merit of this braggart takes—

But for the fear of something worse than death.

In speaking out one loses influence.

The chance for change by pleas and prayers is gone.

The chance to modify the devil's deeds

As critic from within is still my hope.

To quit the club! Be outside looking in!

This outsideness, this unfamiliar land

From which few travelers ever get back in—

It puzzles mind, it paralyzes will,
And makes us rather bear those ills we have
Than fly to others that we know not of.
Security makes cowards of us all.
I fear to break; I'll work within for change.

ROBERT:

MacBird permits no critics from within.
He draws the line and all are forced to toe.
You're with him or against him, get that
    straight.
Your safety, sir, demands his overthrow.

EGG:

No! No, for still he is our President.

ROBERT:

Your President perhaps, but for myself
I had as lief not be alive as be
In awe of such a thing as that . . .

EGG:

               Enough!

ROBERT:

I was born free as he and so were you.
We both have come as close to being chief.
MacBird! MacBird! (*In a crowlike call.*)
      What coarseness in that sound.
The Egg of Head—that name befits the post.

EGG:

Perhaps it's true, but fate has made him king.

ROBERT:

> The fault, dear Egg, is never in our stars
> But in ourselves that we are underlings.

EGG:

> That you do mean me well I have no doubt,
> But what you work me to, alas I fear.

ROBERT:

> Oh, nation that has lost thy breed of men!
> When could we say but now of this great land
> That her far shores encompassed but one man?
> Ye Gods, there was an Egg of Head here once
> That would have dared the devil . . . and yet
>   now . . .

EGG:

> I know you think I'm acting like a toad
> But still I choose the middle of the road.

Blackout.

MacBird's presidential office. On the screen behind his desk is a huge picture of the President. Office is impressively official but includes a rocking chair. On stage is MacBird's CRONY.

CRONY:

You've got it now, just like those weirdos said—
His room, his desk, his thronelike rocking chair.
You live as lord while he's distinctly dead.
Yet Ken O'Dunc alone shall leave an heir.

Enter MAC BIRD *surrounded by his entourage, which includes the same advisors who surrounded Ken O'Dunc.*

MAC BIRD:

What do you mean, "they're all talking"?
Who's talking?

AIDE:

The older one is buttonholing people, telling them all kinds of things.

MAC BIRD:

What do you mean, "all kinds of things"?

45

AIDE:

Well actually, nothing specific. He's just suggesting things.

CRONY:

He really doesn't say anything, but everyone's listening to him.

MAC BIRD:

If there's one thing I can't stand, it's a yellow-bellied hypocrite. If a man's got something to say, let him step right up and say it to your face.

CRONY:

Listen boss, it's only one guy whining a little. He's just a sore loser. Everybody can tell that. What harm can he do?

MAC BIRD:

In this business we all have our enemies. And I know I'm not immune to personal attacks either. But personal attacks are one thing. We're talking about attacks on the President of the United States. The President needs consensus and unity. I love my country and I love her government. I will suffer much slander myself, suffer in silence. But I will not permit attacks upon our President. Do you all understand that?

ALL:

Yes sir. Yes sir.

MAC BIRD:

What about the younger brother?

CRONY:

He's flying to Boston. At least that's what I heard.

MAC BIRD (*distinctly*):

Have I no friends will rid me of these living fears?

SECRETARY *pokes her head in.*

SECRETARY:

The Earl of Warren's here.

MAC BIRD:

Well, send him in.

EARL:

My lord, you sent for me.

MAC BIRD:

I know; sit down.

EARL *sits down;* MAC BIRD *remains standing, pacing, etc.*

My predecessor's death has grieved the nation.

EARL:

Indeed, he was beloved.

MAC BIRD (*gruffly*):

Indeed, quite right.
Now some few folks whose wits are crazed with grief

Still seek a villain, chase a phantom foe.
Although the killer's killed, they cannot rest.
And I desire to set their minds at ease.

EARL:

Small doubts still flit like fleas throughout the
    nation.

MAC BIRD:

That's why I'd like a full investigation,
Conducted by a man of such repute
That we may put an end to all these doubts.
That man is you.

EARL:

                        Oh, cursèd spite
That ever I was born to set things right.

MAC BIRD:

I don't believe you understand the job.
I wouldn't say you're asked to set things *right*.
I think you get the point

EARL:

                        Oh, whine and pout,
That ever I was born to bury doubt.

MAC BIRD:

You get the picture now.

EARL:

                        I can't accept.

MAC BIRD:

Cannot accept? Your nation needs you, boy.

In times of crisis, confidence is key.
Respect for law and leaders guides this land.
If folks suspect their leaders, law breaks down.
You'd help destroy the very law you love.
Just think about those law-abiding folk
That should be sheltered from despair and
    doubt.
Those simple people need their trusting faith.
They count on us to work their problems out.

EARL:

It's too confusing. Let me think it out.

MAC BIRD:

Earl, you and I must tolerate confusion.
We bear this load to save them their illusion.

EARL:

I cannot go against the needs of conscience.

MAC BIRD:

Forget your needs as I forget my own.
Private likes and dislikes must give way.
For their sake, share this load I bear alone.
Your nation is awaiting what you say.

EARL:

This tragic ambiguity makes me hesitant.
But duty wins. I'm with you, Mr. President.

MAC BIRD (*slapping him on back*):
Well, well, I knew that you'd come through.

EARL:

Adieu, MacBird.

MAC BIRD:

So long, you'all.

EARL:

Adieu. (*Exits.*)

MAC BIRD:

A man of honor; mighty rare these days.

SECRETARY *sticks her head in.*

SECRETARY:

The press is here.

MAC BIRD:

Jes' let 'em cool their heels.
(*To self:*) I've got to write this speech to meet
the press.
(*Pacing.*) Now, how do I convey my earnestness,
The agony I suffer silently
While cares of state are tearing me apart;
My deep concern for every living soul,
Contrasted with the grandeur of my vision.
Now, how to make one interview show that . . .

MAC BIRD *becomes absorbed in thinking. At
other end of room two members of his entourage conspire together.*

CRONY:

Did you hear MacBird, the way he said,
"Have I no friends will rid me of this living
fear?"
Wasn't it so?

AIDE:

Those were his very words.

CRONY:

"Have I no friends?" he said, and so distinct;
He said it with a meaning.

AIDE:

That he did.

CRONY:

And saying it, I thought he looked at you
As if to say, "I wish you were that friend
To rid me of this terror in my heart."

AIDE:

He meant, of course, those brothers. Come let's
go.
I am that friend will rid him of his foe. (*Exits.*)

MAC BIRD (*picking up phone*):
Okay, Miss Moya; send the newsmen in.

Newsmen enter chattering. MAC BIRD *shakes
some hands, slaps some backs, etc., then re-
turns to pose at his desk. Noise dies down;
hushes are heard.*

CRONY:

Pipe down, be still. MacBird's about to speak.

Silence. MAC BIRD *rises to his feet.*

MAC BIRD:

A tragic twist of fateful sorrow, friends,
Made me your President that fearful day.

And I shall be the President of all:
Not just the rich, not just the fortunate
Not just the folks who vote for me,
          (*Ominous or emphatic.*) but *all.*
And stretching out beyond our nation's shores,
To East and West around this seething globe,
Where constant conflagrations blaze and rage,
We mean to be the fireman of peace,
Dousing flames with freedom's forceful flow.
Our highest goal is peace, but in its quest
We shall not fear to use our righteous might.
In short, we seek that Pox Americana
That all the Freedom-Loving world desires.
The unity of *all* alone contents us,
We plan to guide this planet by consensus.

Pause. Applause. REPORTERS *raise their hands
and* MAC BIRD *nods to one.*

REPORTER:
Your majesty, how do you view our future?

MAC BIRD:
I'm glad you asked that, Bob—I have a dream.
We have an opportunity to move
Not only toward the rich society,
But upwards toward the Smooth Society.
My Smooth Society has room for all;
For each, a house, a car, a family,
A private psychoanalyst, a dog,
And rows of gardens, neatly trimmed and
     hedged.

This land will be a garden carefully pruned.
We'll lop off any branch that looks too tall,
That seems to grow too lofty or too fast.
And any weed that springs up on our soil,
To choke the plants I've neatly set in rows,
Gets plucked up root and all, by me,
    MacBird—
And this I do for you, my wholesome flowers.
I see a garden blooming undisturbed
Where all the buds are even in their rows.
An ordered garden, sweet with unity,
That is my dream; my Smooth Society.

Applause from REPORTERS *which finally dies down.*

I thank you, gentlemen. Next question, please.

REPORTER:

Your majesty, how do you plan to deal
With rebel groups which thrive in Viet Land?

MAC BIRD:

What rebel groups? Where is this Viet Land?
Who gave them folks permission to rebel?
Lord MacNamara, valiant chief of war,
What is this place I've just been asked about?

MAC NAMARA:

It's way off to the East, eight thousand miles.
A little land we're trying to subdue.

MAC BIRD:

What crap is this "we're *trying* to subdue"?

Since when do we permit an open challenge
To all the world's security and peace?
Rip out those Reds! Destroy them, root and
  branch!
Deploy whatever force you think we need!
Eradicate this noxious, spreading weed!

MAC NAMARA:

Your word is my command. Your will is done.
That land will be subdued ere set of sun.

Exit MAC NAMARA. MAC BIRD *turns back to
press.*

MAC BIRD:

Gentlemen, I thank you all for coming.
You're now dismissed.

ALL:

Thank *you,* your majesty.

REPORTERS *begin to file out. Handshakes; cam-
eras removed, etc. A small cluster gathers.*

1ST REPORTER:

What a shit!

2ND REPORTER:

I guess you've heard the rumors.

1ST REPORTER:

Rumors, hell! I heard him here today.

3RD REPORTER:

The world is gonna be his private garden.
Defoliating weeds and lopping branches.

MAC BIRD *ambles over toward the group*.

2ND REPORTER:
Watch out or you'll be weeded out yourself.

MAC BIRD (*backslapping*):
How'd it go? You know I'm new at this.

REPORTERS:
Oh, fine.

MAC BIRD:
       I hope your story's good enough
So I can ask you *all* back here next time.

They start to move off.

Write it well now.

1ST REPORTER:
       Yes sir-ree.

2ND REPORTER:
          Will do.

MAC BIRD (*calling as they leave*):
My secretary's waiting in the hall
With autographèd photos for you all.

REPORTERS *leave except for one or two at the door.*

By ding! That press confab went off real well.
I hit it off just fine with all the boys.
But editors will twist the story round.
They're all against me viciously, you know.

Enter LADY MAC BIRD *followed by her two* DAUGHTERS. LADY MAC BIRD *is carrying a giant bouquet of flowers. She is distraught. The* DAUGHTERS *carry aerosol cans.* LADY MAC BIRD *sniffs around the room, gasping at a foul odor. She stops at* MAC BIRD.

LADY MAC BIRD:
Here's the smell. Out, out damned odor, out!

DAUGHTERS *press aerosol sprays.*

The smell of blood is still within my nostrils.

MAC BIRD (*tense, whispering to* LADY MAC BIRD):
My dearest sparrow, cut this nonsense out!

DAUGHTER 1:
She's been this way or worse for several days
now.

DAUGHTER 2:
We have to follow after her with Air-Wick,
For every several steps she stops and sniffs
And crying out, "There's blood upon this
spot!",
She makes us spray to mask the phantom smell.

DAUGHTER 1:
And everywhere she goes, she carries flowers.

DAUGHTER 2:
The rooms are sickly sweet with perfumed
plants.

DAUGHTER 1:
  I think our mother's finally flipped her lid.

  LADY MAC BIRD *has been wandering around the room.*

LADY MAC BIRD (*distractedly*):
  Flowers by the roadside . . .
                    plant these flowers . . .
  Let all the land be lined with living blooms.
  Yet all the petals of a summer's roses
  Can never sweeten this accursèd land.

MAC BIRD:
  Be calm, sweet bird. She's often like this . . .
    nerves . . .
  To ease your frenzied wits, we will decree
  That all our highways shall be lined with
    flowers.
  We all applaud the lofty dedication
  With which you seek to beautify our nation.

  Pushing LADY MAC BIRD *out with* DAUGHTERS.

  And now sweet woodchuck, charming chicka-
    dees,
  Go chirping off and tend your household
    chores.

  LADY MAC BIRD *exits, and her sighs and excla-
  mations, along with whish of Air-Wick, are
  heard off-stage.* MAC BIRD *sinks down at the
  desk with discouragement.* MAC NAMARA *enters
  excitedly.*

MAC NAMARA:
> MacBird!

MAC BIRD:
>> Good God, what's next?

MAC NAMARA:
>>> The matter's urgent.
> It's touching on our war in Viet Land.
> That pacifying program we embarked on
> Did not compel surrender, as we hoped.
> A new approach is desperately required.

MAC BIRD:
> Are we, or are we not, the strongest power?

MAC NAMARA:
> Of course we are.

MAC BIRD:
>> Then why this blabbering?

MAC NAMARA:
> Yes sir, but we've run into complications
> Which must be settled soon.

MAC BIRD (*sigh*):
>> Then come with me.

They walk together toward exit.

> I git to be a-weary o' this show
> And wish my country didn't need me so.

SCENE THREE

A street in front of Bobby's residence. Two of his
AIDES *are heading toward his house, dressed con-*
spiratorially in trench coats, hats low over eyes.

AIDE 1:

> Who else will be at Bobby's house this eve-
> ning?

AIDE 2:

> Some senators, a congressman and us.
> Last night he met with unionists and press,
> This morning with the independent right,
> Tomorrow come the leaders of the left.
> He wisely speaks to each group separately.

AIDE 1:

> Have all agreed to join our enterprise?

AIDE 2:

> The Negro leaders say their flocks are wary,
> But then of course, they've no place else to go.
> The southern racists think MacBird a traitor,
> And so may not impede his overthrow.
> Some fear the widening war, while others say
> He's meddling with our military stands.
> All fear his one-man rule, his arrogance;
> His secret slaughters stink upon his hands.

And Bobby is the man who can unite
The tyrant's foes, though they be left or right.

They knock on Robert's door; ROBERT *and* TED
step cautiously outside.

TED:

Shhh, the house is bugged.

ROBERT:

Let's stay out here.

AIDE 2:

How goes it, Bobby?

AIDE 1:

Which ones have agreed?

AIDE 2:

What firm commitments have we to our cause?

ROBERT:

It's going just as well as we could hope,
No worse, no better; naturally they hedge.
Yet certain major groups are lined up firm.

TED:

Tonight we've got the wishy-washy liberals.

AIDE 1:

We've got to stress the threat he is to *them*.
These congressmen must see that he'll destroy
Their liberties—make them of no more voice
Than dogs that are so often beat for barking
Though they are kept to do so.

TED:

> Heat them up.
Remind them of their ancient sovereignties
Which now are trampled under by MacBird.

ROBERT:

Heat not the furnace for our foes so hot
That it may singe ourselves. For if we win,
Then *we* will have to temper this fierce heat.

Enter CONGRESSMAN *and two* SENATORS.

TED:

Who's there?

SENATOR 1:

> It's us.

ROBERT:

> It's safe, I know the voice.

They draw near. Handshakes, etc.

I think you know each other, gentlemen.
You know the solemn purpose of our meeting.

CONGRESSMAN:

I also know MacBird is waxing strong.
His warpèd roots are spreading in the earth.
Thus planted firm he sucks the soil's fertility
And any green and tender shoot's choked out.

SENATOR 1:

It's all too true. I heard about your brother.

AIDE 1:

> What news is this? Has Teddy met with ill?

TED:

> I thought you knew. Last week my airplane crashed.
> A most peculiar failure in the engine.
> (*Throws aside his cloak, revealing an arm in a cast.*)

ROBERT:

> MacBird mailed out a wreath immediately.

TED:

> But me, I merely broke a bone or two.

SENATOR 1:

> He's strong and wicked. None of us can stop him.

SENATOR 2:

> I see our nation sink beneath her yoke.
> She weeps, she bleeds, and each new day a gash
> Is added to her wounds.

ROBERT:

> Then bleed, poor land!
> Great tyranny has dug his roots too firm,
> For no one here dares check him.

TED:

> No, not true!

SENATOR 2:

> Or else why are we here?

ROBERT:

Your words revive my spirits, gentlemen.

Galloping hoofbeats are heard off-stage. A few bars of the "William Tell Overture."

AIDE 1:
Who comes so fast?

TED:

I see the Wayne of Morse.

WAYNE OF MORSE *strides in rapidly, wearing Quixote armor and carrying lance.*

ROBERT:
An unexpected though most welcome guest.

WAYNE:

Forgive this rash intrusion. I have come
Because I cannot stand this nation's war.
MacBird's gone mad, a killer turned berserk.
Each morn new widows' wails, new orphan
    cries
Howl up to heaven.

TED:

I grant him bloody,
Arrogant, avaricious, false, vindictive,
Smacking of every sin that has a name;
And yet the war itself, without his villainy,
May have to be more brutal than we hoped.

ROBERT:
I basically agree with both positions.

Regardless of the war, one thing is certain—
This man's not fit to rule in war or peace.
We all agree to that.

WAYNE:

        Fit to govern!
Nay, not fit to live! Oh, nation miserable,
With an untitled tyrant, bloody-sceptred,
When shalt thou see thy wholesome days again?

ROBERT:

We've met to help restore our land to health.
Let's swear to her our resolution now,
That we shall cut this canker from her flesh,
This tyrant whose name alone blisters our
    tongues.

TED:

Let's swear, let's swear!

AIDE 2:

        Our hearts, our hands are yours.

ROBERT:

Give me your hands, each of you, one by one.

They shake all around.

TED:

I swear!

SENATOR 2:

    I swear!

CONGRESSMAN:

        And here's my solemn oath.

SENATOR 2:

About the Egg of Head, should we sound him?

CONGRESSMAN:

Let us not leave him out.

SENATOR 1:

No, by no means.

AIDE 1:

Oh, let us have him, for his silver tongue
Can purchase us the purest reputation
And buy approval for most any deed.

WAYNE:

Why mention it? He'll never go along.

SENATOR 2:

I would have said the same a week ago,
And yet I have a friend who heard him say
He could no longer keep his silent vow,
But he must speak, and for the very cause
The Wayne of Morse is stirred—that is, these
	wars.

AIDE 2:

It's said within this coming week he means
To rise and break in public from MacBird.

AIDE 1:

I've heard the same.

WAYNE:

I know it can't be true.
Oh, what a rogue and peasant slave is he!

Is it not monstrous how he bows and begs?
He lives but in a fiction, in a dream,
Wherein he plays the hero. But awake,
A dull and muddy-mettled fellow he.
He plays the puppet, jigging on the stage;
He jumps for any hand that pulls the strings.

SENATOR 2:
No, no, you're wrong! I've got it from my
source;
He'll speak this week.

WAYNE:

Alas, it can't be true.

A messenger has come in and handed a note to ROBERT.

ROBERT:
What's this? (*Scans.*) He might have spoken
up before.
The Egg of Head is gone; he'll speak no more.

ROBERT *passes the note to* CONGRESSMAN.

CONGRESSMAN (*scanning note*):
"He dropped down in the street," the message
says.
"The press was quick to call it heart attack,
And yet the rumor goes that near the body,
A poison dart was found."

TED:

Oh, villainy!

SENATOR 2:
   The Egg of Head is gone.

ROBERT:
                        Be comforted.
   Let's make a potion of our great revenge
   To cure the deadly grief.

SENATOR 1:
                        Alas, he's gone.

ROBERT:
   Make this the whetstone of your swords. Let
      grief
   Convert to anger. Don't blunt your heart,
      enrage it.

SENATOR 1:
   He hasn't touched us yet, but who is next?

TED:
   Oh, villain, traitor, cur.

AIDE 2:
                  Alas, poor country!
   It can't be called our mother, but our grave
   Where no one but the ignorant feels safe.

WAYNE:
   Where sighs and groans and shrieks that rend
      the air
   Are all unheard by men who dare not hear.
   This violent discord seems the modern tune.

The bloody hand that plucks our flowers here
Is ravishing the fields in Viet Land.
Oh, carnal, bloody, and unnatural act!
The accidental bombing, casual slaughters!

CONGRESSMAN:
Tsk, tsk.

SENATOR 2:
He's right.

TED:
It's got to end somewhere.

WAYNE:
I must be off. I have to make a speech in
Some college town where someone's planned a
teach-in.
I'm off to fight the war.

ALL:
Adieu.

WAYNE:
Farewell. (*Exits.*)

CONGRESSMAN:
A bit of an extremist, I would say.

ROBERT:
I think that we can use him anyway.

Enter MESSENGER.

MESSENGER:

Another plot against your brother's life
His yacht's been tampered with—these bolts
   sawed off.
Had this gone undiscovered—

TED:

Woe are we!

ROBERT:

But once again you'll merely break some bones.

SENATOR 2 (*to* BOBBY):
You may be next, I fear.

AIDE 1:

You know his nature,
Jealous and aggressive. We've seen his sword;
Its edge is sharp; it's long and reaches far,
And where it won't extend he still can dart it.

TED:

Take my advice, let's flee beyond his reach.

ROBERT:

I'm now prepared for exile in the East,
But there I mean to organize my troops,
And with my force of liberals from New York,
I shall return to make that fat bird squawk.

*Trumpet blast, hurrahs and handshakes. Exit
all but* ROBERT *and* TED.

The meeting went off fairly well.

TED:

> Yes, quite.

ROBERT:

They're in our pocket, when the time is right.

Blackout.

ACT THREE

Scene One

Stage is dark.

MAC BIRD:

Arrest them all!

Lights come up on MacBird's office. Chants of demonstrators from off-stage. Enter MAC BIRD *and* CRONY.

I said arrest them all!

CRONY:

There's news, more news!

MAC BIRD:

Spit out your spiteful news.

CRONY:

Peace paraders marching.

MAC BIRD:

Stop 'em!

CRONY:

Beatniks burning draft cards.

MAC BIRD:

Jail 'em!

CRONY:

Negroes starting sit-ins.

MAC BIRD:

> Gas 'em!

CRONY:
Latin rebels rising.

MAC BIRD:

> Shoot 'em!

CRONY:
Asian peasants arming.

MAC BIRD:

> Bomb 'em!

CRONY:
Congressmen complaining.

MAC BIRD:

> Fuck 'em!

Flush out this filthy scum; destroy dissent.
It's treason to defy your President.

CRONY *hesitates.*

You heard me! Go on, get your ass in gear.
Get rid of all this protest stuff, y'hear?

CRONY *scurries off-stage.* MAC BIRD *is alone.*

My God, my God, has everyone forsaken me?

Enter LADY MAC BIRD.

LADY MAC BIRD:
My lord, to bed?

MAC BIRD:

You know I dare not sleep.

LADY MAC BIRD:

Forgive me, I forgot your malady.
My lord, the land's beset by evil omens.
The light is dark, the dark is darkly lit.
Last night the Eastern Kingdom blackened
    over.
The people feared a failure of the power,
And prophets cried with not-too-hidden
    meaning
That he with greatest power dwelt in darkness,
And darkness would descend upon his nation.
But in the black, more dreadful than the
    darkness,
There gleamed demonic flames and dire
    combustion.
A flickering draft card burned, and then a
    draft board.
Then horror, horror, horror, howling horror!
A human being set itself ablaze.
It blazed and cursed thy name and blazed and
    cursed,
And then it dimmed, and yet they saw it still.
Although 'twas dark, the flames had seared
    their eyeballs.
They say they see it still. It blazed and cursed.
It cursed thy name. O God, O God, forgive us!

MAC BIRD:

I know, alas, our folk are superstitious.

They're simple souls that see in black and
    white.
And so to ease their doubts and foolish fancies,
I plan to call a national day of prayer.
We'll get the biggest preacher in the country.
You know the one I mean—the guy's got class.
We'll make it high-toned, dignified, and
    solemn;
Organs, choirs, pictures of me, ponderin'.
Now that's the sort of thing builds confidence.

LADY MAC BIRD:
    I just don't know . . .

MAC BIRD:
                    I gotta hand it to me.
    I sure got style. MacBird, you're so damn
        sharp.

LADY MAC BIRD:
    Then pray for me, my lord.

MAC BIRD:
                    Of course, of course!
    But now tonight I'll see those three weird
        critters
    That prophesied so truly of my fate.
    Though they be fiends, no matter what the
        source,
    I must be certain in my future course.

Scene Two

Spooky setting with caldron at one side of stage. Enter WITCHES *who dance around caldron to eerie music.* ROBERT *enters from other side of stage and wanders across searching for something.* WITCHES *huddle behind caldron and music stops.*

1ST WITCH:
He's seeking us.

2ND WITCH:
Hush up, I think he heard.

3RD WITCH:
We'll see him next, but first let's meet Mac-Bird.

2ND WITCH:
You're certain that he'll find us?

3RD WITCH:
It's arranged.

1ST WITCH:
Then let's prepare the brew till he appears.

More music. They circle around the caldron, then chant.

Round about the caldron go,
Watch the bubbles boil and grow.

Stench of Strong and tongue of Kerr,
Picket, sit-in, strike, and stir.
Regents raging, Reagan hot,
All boil up our protest pot.

ALL:

Bubble and bubble, toil and trouble,
Burn baby burn, and caldron bubble.

2ND WITCH:

Round the caldron chant and sing,
Arson, rape, and rioting.
Bombed-out church and burning cross
In the boiling caldron toss.
Club and gas and whip and gun,
Niggers strung up just for fun.
Black men beat and burnt and shot,
Bake within our melting pot.

ALL:

> Bubble and bubble, toil and trouble,
> *Burn baby burn,* and caldron bubble.

3RD WITCH:

> Taylor's tongue and Goldberg's slime,
> MacNamara's bloody crime
> Sizzling skin of napalmed child,
> Roasted eyeballs, sweet and mild.
> Now we add a fiery chunk
> From a burning Buddhist monk.
> Flaming field and blazing hut,
> Infant fingers cooked and cut,
> Young man's heart and old man's gut,
> Groin and gall and gore of gook
> In our caldron churn and cook.

ALL:

> Bubble and bubble, toil and trouble,
> *Burn baby burn,* and caldron bubble.

> *More eerie music and dancing. Then a sudden stop.*

2ND WITCH:

> By the pricking of my thumbs,
> Something wicked this way comes.

> *Enter* MAC BIRD.

MAC BIRD:

> How now, you secret, black, and midnight fiends?
> What are you at?

ALL:

A deed without a name.

MAC BIRD:

I order you by all authority!
No matter how you know it, answer me!
I must find out.

1ST WITCH:

Command!

2ND WITCH:

Demand!

3RD WITCH:

Speak out!

MAC BIRD:

What must I fear? How steady is my throne?
Can any force effect my overthrow?
I'm bent to know by the worst means the worst.
Speak out, you fiends, although your tongues
    be cursed!

The WITCHES *pass around a mug filled with
the brew.*

ALL WITCHES:

Darkest matters must we settle.
Boil and bubble, answer kettle!

VOICE *from caldron speaks. Image of General
Ky comes forth.*

VOICE:

Be bloody, bold and resolute, MacBird;

All cautious counsel scorn, for be it known,
No man with beating heart or human blood
Shall ever harm MacBird or touch his throne.

MAC BIRD:

Then Bobby, live! What fear have I from thee?
And yet I'll make assurance double sure,
That I may tell pale-hearted fear it lies,
That I may sleep at night, you shall not live.

1ST WITCH:

The caldron boils again. There's more to hear.

VOICE *from caldron speaks. Image of Madame Nu comes forth.*

VOICE:

Be iron fisted, proud, and take no care
Who chafes or frets or where conspirers are.
MacBird shall never, never be undone
Till burning wood doth come to Washington.

MAC BIRD:

What means this "burning wood"?

WITCHES *start moving off.*

                            Wait, tell me more!

2ND WITCH:

Adieu MacBird, we must at once depart . . .

3RD WITCH:

To meet with one who also heeds our art.

WITCHES *glide off.*

MAC BIRD:

"Till burning wood doth come to Washing-
    ton."
It makes no sense. But that's of no account,
For I have understood the clearer part,
And now I fear no foe with human heart.

Exit MAC BIRD. *Re-enter* WITCHES.

3RD WITCH:

By the twitching of my ears
Something cunning this way steers.

Enter ROBERT.

1ST WITCH:

All hail, young Bob! All hail the Senator!

2ND WITCH:

All hail, young Bob, that shall be—

ROBERT:

                    Cut it short.
No wordy welcomes. There's no time to flatter.
Just give me facts; I work with data.
Speak if you can. What news have you for me?

3RD WITCH:

I could a tale unfold whose lightest word
Would harrow up thy soul, freeze thy young
    blood,
Make thy two eyes, like stars, start from their
    spheres,

Thy knotted and combinèd locks to part
And each particular hair to stand on end.
If thou didst ever thy dear brother love,
Mark now my every word. List, list, oh, list!
The serpent that did sting thy brother's life
Now wears his crown!

ROBERT:

Oh, you pathetic soul!
I'm no prince Hamlet, nor was meant to be.
Your fantasy I know to be a fact.
I live not in a fiction nor a dream.
I have the proof and I intend to act.
I ask you but to help me set the scene.

1ST WITCH:
Help you set the scene?

ROBERT:

Yea, I have heard
That guilty creatures, sitting at a play
Have by the very cunning of the scene
Been struck so to the quick, that in a fright
They have revealed their malefactions.
Tomorrow night MacBird will host a banquet,
And so I have prepared a little play
In which you wound him first, then stay on
　　stage
And play your rightful roles behind my throne.

1ST WITCH:
Help you set *your* scene?

2ND WITCH:

>Not on your life.

3RD WITCH:

>We ne'er shall help prepare thy prancing
>> entrance,
>We ne'er shall fetch the conquering Caesar in,
>Nor shall we set the scene of thy ascension.

1ST WITCH:

>We'll help you with your exit, if you like.

ROBERT (*suspicious and angry*):

>What are your parts and parties? What are
>you?

WITCHES:

>Players.

ROBERT:

>Players, eh? (*To* 2ND WITCH:) Say, fella, can
>you sing?

2ND WITCH:

>Can I sing? I *loves* to entertain folks.
>(*Singing with a leer, constantly watching* ROB-
>ERT *to see if he is upset:*)
>Massa makes de darkies love him,
>Cause he was so kind.
>Now dey sadly weep above him,
>Mourning cause he leave dem behind.
>Down in de cornfield,
>Hear dat mournful sound,

> All de darkies am a weeping,
> Massa's in de cold, cold ground.

1ST WITCH:
> He has not changed his color, shows no tears.
> Pray you, no more—your music missed its
> mark.

ROBERT:
> Can you sing that song tomorrow evening?

2ND WITCH:
> I sing when I'm so moved.

ROBERT:
> We'll have it tomorrow night. You could for a
> need study a verse of some twelve or sixteen
> lines, which I could set down and insert in it,
> could you not?

2ND WITCH:
> Man, we write our *own* lines. Screw your script.

3RD WITCH:
> We're self-employed, free-enterprising spirits.
> We're not in any politician's pay.

ROBERT:
> Never mind, insert what words you will.
> Any lines you like, any phrase you fancy,
> Any play you write will in the end advance me.

Scene Three

The convention hall. Sounds of drums and fife in distance. Enter alone two SENATORS. ROBERT *stands alone upstage.*

SENATOR 1:
    The liberal power is near, led on by Robert.
    The lords of Eastern Industry and Banks,
    With blazoned shields, are riding at the head.
    The union men are marching in the ranks
    And Negro troops are bringing up the rear.

SENATOR 2:
    And what about the tyrant? Where is he?

SENATOR 1:
    He fortifies himself with new decrees.
    Last month he made it law for congressmen
    That they could say no more than yea or nay
    And only vote on matters he'd present.
    And furthermore he's censored all the press;
    And here at this convention, as you know,
    He's having many delegates thrown out.
    I just found out he's changed the voting rules.
    Now votes are given by the *size* of state.

SENATOR 2:
    Some say he's mad. Others who hate him less

Have called his meg'lomaniac decrees
A zealousness for order. But for certain
He cannot buckle his distended pouch
Within the belt of rule.

SENATOR 1:

                Now can he smell
His bloody murders reeking on his hands.
Now hourly revolts disturb his reign.
Those he commands move only in command
And none in love. Now does he feel his title
Hanging loose about him like a giant's robe
Upon a dwarfish thief.

SENATOR 2:

                Well, let's be off
To give our votes where they are truly owed.
MacBird has made us swallow bitter pills.
Strong medicines must cure the nation's ills.

They move toward ROBERT, *engaging him in conversation.*

SENATOR 1:
The list of allies lengthens every hour.

SENATOR 2:
The center left-wing caucus is assured.

SENATOR 1:
And at the opening session in the morning
I know the southern states will be secured.

SENATOR 2:

> I haven't done a tally but I'm certain
> We're even now beyond the needed votes.

SENATOR 1:

> I'm sure MacBird must be preparing some-
>   thing;
> He can't just let the power slip away.

SENATOR 2:

> Oh no, he's unaware of any problem.

SENATOR 1:

> Could be. In fact I know that he was planning
> A huge pre-victory party here tonight.

ROBERT:

> I've heard about that slated celebration.

SENATOR 1:

> The king doth wake tonight to take his rouse
> 'Twixt swaggering, and stuffing food, and
>   dancing
> He'll loudly swill his draughts of whisky down.

ROBERT:

> This heavy-handed revel I'll attend
> And there perform a phantom pantomime
> To undermine the last remaining friend
> Who still believes MacBird controls his mind.
> Convention eve, and now the play's the thing
> Wherein I'll catch the conscience of the king.

Exit all three.

Scene Four

MacBird's hotel room. The atmosphere is something between a western saloon and an Elizabethan tavern, with a player piano providing music. Mac-Bird's followers are scattered around playing poker, etc. Enter MAC BIRD, *jovial, swinging a* DAUGHTER *on each arm, amidst ya-hooing.* CRONY *follows along behind. Lots of circulating, jolly carryings-on.*

MAC BIRD:
> Be seated, friends. You know your own degrees.
> From first to last, to all a hearty howdy.
> Ourselves will mingle in your company
> And play the humble host.

CRONY (*whispering furtively*):
>   Your majesty?

MAC BIRD (*ignoring* CRONY):
> Alas, our lovely lady keeps her state
> But bids me say her heart declares you
>   welcome.

CRONY (*still hovering over him*):
> Your majesty?

MAC BIRD:
>   More lists? Oh, get you gone!
> (*Turning back to guests.*)

89

I'll sit here in your midst, betwixt you all.
Be large in mirth! Anon we'll drink a measure.

CRONY:

Your majesty, your majesty, please look.

MAC BIRD:

Get out of here and take your lying lists!
I'll hear no more about your damned defectors!
Bring on the booze, the whisky, and the beer!
This is a victory party, do ya hear?

Music sounds, drinks are passed round, MAC-BIRD does a little cutting up and some ya-hoos.

Now this is more the style. Another round!
More like, my lords. God bless this merry sight,
And good digestion wait on appetite.
The food!

Huge platters of roast meat are brought in, everyone gathers round them. Lots of pushing and stuffing food. Finally they all settle down in their places—a little quiet spell, all with full mouths.

Be silent all. This here's a solemn moment.
A toast, my lords, to our departed king.
Oh, what a grace was seated on that brow!
You all know how I loved him; honored him.
An eye like Mars to threaten and command,
An angel's locks, the face of Jove himself.
I held him as a hero, as a God.

I'm sure you all know that, but think on
this . . .
This counterfeit presentment of a brother.
That great grown serpent shed, has left a
worm.
A lion to a lynx are these two brothers.
A lynx, coyote, bobcat, desert rat!
The love I bear our dear departed king,
That love hath made me vow his younger
brother
Shall not be left to soil his sacred name.
(*Getting hysterical.*)
You know how much I loved him. Lords you
know,
You know, you know, you know, you know my
love
My love, my love, my love, my love, you know.

The WITCHES *have entered silently and un-
noticed during the toast. While* MAC BIRD
speaks the 2ND WITCH *deliberately, and in an
ominous manner, removes his mask and puts
on white gloves, spats, a skimmer hat, and carefully applies white minstrel lips to his face.
The other witches put on skimmers, celluloid
collars, etc.*

DAUGHTER 1:
Stay seated sirs. Our Dad is often thus.
The fit is of a moment. It'll pass.

MAC BIRD:

My grief is deep, It floods when left to flow.
But smile my lords. Let's have a little show.
Entertainers! Send on the entertainers!

WITCHES *leap on dais. The* 1ST WITCH *plays a knee-slapping rhythm on a banjo and the* 3RD WITCH *rattles a tambourine. They do a soft-shoe and some "walk-around steps."* MAC BIRD *is obviously delighted and drinks heartily.*

2ND WITCH (*singing in minstrel style to "Massa's in de Cold, Cold, Ground"*):
Massa makes de darkies love him
Cause he was so kind.
Now dey sadly weep above him
Mourning cause he leaves dem behind.

How he loved his darkies dearly;
Used to shake my hand.
Now de world am sad and dreary
Massa's in anodder land.

2ND WITCH:
Mr. Interlocutor, Mr. Interlocutor!

1ST WITCH:
Yes, Mr. Bones?

2ND WITCH:
Mr. Interlocutor, hab you heard about dat sweet liddle birdie dat am gwine to hab a chile?

1ST WITCH:
What little bird is that, Mr. Bones?

2ND WITCH:
Why de President's liddle girl. She gwine to get married right away.

1ST WITCH:
What are they going to call the child when it's born, Mr. Bones?

2ND WITCH:
Dey gwine to call it Early Bird. Yeah!

Chorus: Ober de nation
Hear dat mournful sound
Chickens coming home and roosting
Massa's in de cold cold ground.

Round de nation am a ringing
De darkies' mournful song
While de Macky Bird am singing
Happy as de day is long.

Where de orange flame am blazing
By de grassy mound.
Dere old Massa am a lazing
Sleeping in de cold cold ground.

Chorus: Repeat.

When de winter snow was falling,
When de days were long,
We could hear ol' Massa calling
Cause he was so young and strong.

Now de cherry trees am blooming
At his old front door.
Now de summer days am coming
Massa nebber calls no more.

Chorus: Repeat.

Shouts.

Everyone sing! Follow the bouncing ball.

*The words of the Chorus appear on the screen
with a bouncing ball.*

ALL:
Chorus: Repeat.

MAC BIRD:
Fie! Foul stuff! Bring on another act!

Come, something rousing! Send us something
   live!

MAC BIRD *turns to fill his drink and chuck his*
DAUGHTER *under the chin. The* WITCHES *parade
off the dais.* ROBERT *has entered and stands
alone on the dais. Only he and* MAC BIRD *are lit.*
MAC BIRD *turns back to face the dais. He sees
the figure of* KEN O'DUNC *and panics.*

Thou cans't not say I did it. Damn your eyes!

DAUGHTER:
   What folly is this, father? Lords, sit down.

MAC BIRD:
   You dare not say t'was I—There was a time
   That when the brains were out the man would
      die,
   And there's an end. But now they rise again.
   Avaunt and quit my sight! Let the earth hide
      thee!
   Thy bones are marrowless, thy blood is cold,
   Thou hast no mortal vision in those eyes
   Which thou dost turn on me.

DAUGHTER:
                        Oh stay, my lords.
   (*To* MAC BIRD:)
   Why do you make such movement? When all's
      done
   You look but on a guest.

MAC BIRD:

What men dare, I dare.
Approach thou like the rugged Russian bear,
The hundred-headed dragon of the east,
Take any shape but *that* and my firm nerves
Shall never tremble. Or be alive again
And dare me to the showdown with thy Colt.

ROBERT:

Mark me, MacBird. Tomorrow we shall meet.

"High Noon" music rising.

And damned be he that first cries out "retreat."

ROBERT *turns on his heel and exits slowly.*

MAC BIRD:

Come back, you fiend! Hence, horrid
hellhound!
Unreal mockery, hence! Why so he's gone.
I am the king again!

*Lights come up. The guests are staring dum-
founded at* MAC BIRD. *They begin moving off.*

Stay here! Sit still!

They continue moving.

Then I'll sit down. Give me some wine. Fill
full.
I drink the general joy of all my guests.
And to our former king, whom we do miss.
Would he were here. To all and him we thirst.

And to you fools who fled . . . Your souls be
cursed!

The guests have all left now. DAUGHTERS *help*
MAC BIRD *stagger off. Three* WITCHES *are left on*
stage.

2ND WITCH:
I'll drink to that myself.

3RD WITCH:
O wondrous scene!

1ST WITCH:
I found it low, pathetic, and obscene.

3RD WITCH:
How true. MacBird's too easy to attack.
By now he's scoffed and sneered at left and
right.
He's so despised it's fash'nable in fact
To call him villain, tweak him by the nose
Break with his party and jeer him in the press.

2ND WITCH:
That bilious Bird!

3RD WITCH:
How popular to say.
But we don't wag as tail behind the mass.
Our role is to expand their consciousness.
We must expose this subtle Bobcat's claws;
He even now collects the straying sheep
And nudges them so gently toward the fold.

O sheep, awake and flee this fenced corral.
He's just like all the rest. They're all alike.

2ND WITCH:

Yeah, white politicians. They all look alike.

1ST WITCH:

And they all wanna help, "but of course it
takes time."

2ND WITCH:

Yes it sure does take time while they're warm
and well fed
And they sit on their backsides while my ass
gets whipped.
It sure does take time, but I'm startin' to see
That they'll *stop* kickin' me when it *starts*
hurtin' them.
Damn this prayin' and pleadin' and non-
violent slime.
I'm off my knees; man, you've used up your
time.

3RD WITCH:

When the blood burns, how plentif'lly the
passion
Lends the tongue vows. These blazes, son,
That give more heat than light, extinguish
both.
Be somewhat scanty with your raging rants.
To serve our cause we channel sentiments.
And these few precepts in thy memory keep.

Be thou militant but by no means adven-
turist . . .

1st witch:
We know, we know.

2nd witch:
We've heard it all before.

3rd witch:
But this above all: to thine own cause be true.
Set sentiment aside and organize.
It is the cause. It is the cause . . .

2nd witch:
My ass.

3rd witch:
Less militant mouthings. More substantial
study
Of revolutions. History teaches us . . .
I'll show you real revolts . . . *(Begins to lift
lantern.)*

2nd witch:
Your light is fading.

3rd witch:
Behold the great rebellions of the past.

2nd witch:
If you can't use it, give that thing to me.
(Grabs lantern.)
Turn off the lights!

(*Stage lights go out.*)
And then turn on the light!

*He hurls the lantern at the back wall. It
smashes. Flames shoot up and spread throughout the theater.*

I'm through with your snubs and I'm through
    with your spurn.
I'm through with you, whitey—so burn, baby,
    burn!

Blackout, but the flames persist.

SCENE FIVE

Robert's convention headquarters. ROBERT *and his followers, including* TED, *are on stage.*

ROBERT:
My friends, I hope the days are near at hand
Of safety and stability.

AIDE 1:
They are, for sure.

CONGRESSMAN:
Which brings to mind the question of new posts
When all MacBird's accomplices are banished.

SENATOR 1:
The matter has been troubling me, as well.

ROBERT:
My worthy lords, I'm mindful of your merit.
Your loyalty will reap you rich rewards.

TED:
Can I head up the Navy? I love boats.

ROBERT:
We shan't discuss it all in detail yet.

Sirens heard in distance. Enter MESSENGER.

101

What news? What news? Has the dictator made
  his move?

MESSENGER:

The news is still the same. The confident
  tyrant
Remains in his hotel suite and will stay
Till we bring all our forces to the vote.

TED (*at window*):
A fire! Bobby! Look, I see a fire!

ROBERT:
Teddy, please, enough!
(*To followers, beginning speech:*) The time
  approaches . . .

TED:
The very biggest fire I ever saw.

ROBERT:
The time approaches which will let us know
What votes we have in hand and what we owe.
The time's at hand, so march we toward our
  fate.
There are some issues force must arbitrate.

Sound of drums and trumpets. ROBERT *marches
off leading his force, with banners, flags, etc.*

The convention floor. Enter MAC BIRD *and a few fol-lowers. Flourish of drum and trumpet as they march in carrying furled banners, balloons, etc.*

MAC BIRD:
>Unfurl our banners, loosen our balloons!
>Blow horns, crack cymbals, cheer, and demon-
>   strate!
>My name in nomination is enough.
>Those three that know all mortal destiny
>Have told me thus, "Fear not, MacBird, fear
>   not,
>No man of heart and blood shall touch your
>   throne."
>Then fly, false friends, fly, fly, desert in droves.
>I fear no foe; I shall not turn and run
>Till burning wood does come to Washington.

Enter MESSENGER.

>More news? What news?

MESSENGER:
>Two hundred votes are gone.

MAC BIRD:
>Two hundred votes are gone? What's that to
>   me?

Go hide your head, you lily-livered loon!
What states defected?

MESSENGER:

All the Eastern Coast.

MAC BIRD:
Get out of here, you fool! Oh, jealousy!
Because I do bestride this narrow world like a
    Colossus,
These petty men who crawl beneath my legs
Turn up their envious eyes at my great
    prowess.
Of course, they hate the hand that holds things
    firm.
Of course, they fear the fist that gets things
    done.
But, most of all, the love the people bear me
Sears deep the jealous hearts of underlings.
Because the cheering crowds would crown me
    king,
Those icy politicians in their spite
Now hiss and scratch and spit and claw me
    down.

Enter CRONY.

CRONY:
My lord, I've come to tell you what I saw
But don't know how to say it.

MAC BIRD:

Out with it!

CRONY:

As I was watching from this hotel roof,
I gazed with wonder down into the streets
While savage blacks rampaging down below
With shrieks of joy set every cherry tree
In Washington aflame.

MAC BIRD:

Liar and slave!

CRONY:

Abuse me as you will, but still it's so.
From out this very window, look yourself.
I say the city burns.

MAC BIRD:

If this is false,
I'll string you up alive. And if it's true,
Then do the same for me. For I begin
To fear the equivocation of those fiends
Who lie with truth—"Fear not till burning
    wood
To Washington does come." And now the
    wood
Of Washington's ablaze. Call out the troops!
If what they say is true, it doth appear
There is no flying hence nor tarrying here.
And yet I'll stay and fight this bloody race.
Bribe, blackmail, bully, and attack!
At least I'll die with harness on my back.

*Sound of trumpets and drums. Robert's forces
enter, in arms, with banners.*

ROBERT:

Now near enough we'll launch the main
attack.

WAYNE:

A rushing torrent of blood which he has spilled
Now hurls him up to dash upon the rocks.

ROBERT:

We'll force the vote and win the race tonight;
Let us be beaten if we dare not fight.

ALL (*shouting*):

On, on, on to the floor fight!

*Robert's force advances across the convention
floor toward MacBird's party.*

ROBERT:

Turn, tyrant, turn.

MAC BIRD:

Of all my foes I fear this twirp the least
But get thee back for the love I bore your
      brother.
On his account I'm loath to do thee harm.

ROBERT:

I'll waste no words, you pompous hypocrite.
The floor fight will undo you on the spot.
And all who would be spared now flee his side,
For mercy pleas shall henceforth be denied.

MAC BIRD:

Don't blow away your breath, you two-bit
      punk.

Your older brother can't protect you here.
I have a charmed career. Now be it known
No man with beating heart or human blood
Can ever harm MacBird or touch his throne.

ROBERT:
Your charm is cursed. Prepare to hear the
worst.
At each male birth, my father in his wisdom
Prepared his sons for their envisaged greatness.
Our first gasped cries as moist, inverted infants
Confirmed for him our place as lords and
leaders.
To free his sons from paralyzing scruples
And temper us for roles of world authority
Our pulpy human hearts were cut away.
And in their place, precision apparatus
Of steel and plastic tubing was inserted.
The sticky, humid blood was drained and then
A tepid antiseptic brine injected.
Although poor Teddy suffered complications,
The operation worked on all the others,
Thus steeling us to rule as more than men.
And so, MacBird, that very man you fear,
Your heartless, bloodless foe now lifts his spear.

ROBERT *slowly raises and aims his spear, but
before he can hurl it,* MAC BIRD *clutches his
heart.*

MAC BIRD:
My heart, my heart! (*Staggers.*)
                    Thus cracks a noble heart!

Falls dead. ROBERT *drops his weapon and doffs his armor. Showing great distress he runs to* MAC BIRD.

ROBERT:

My lords, black sorrow hovers o'er the land.
MacBird, our brilliant leader, lives no more.
The plotters of his downfall, now obscure,
I vow to bring to light, to bring to trial.

Crowd gathers round.

A tragic twist of fateful sorrow, friends,
Makes me your President this fearful day.
And though I never sought it, history
Assigned to me her most demanding task,
To follow my great predecessor's path
In hewing out the Smooth Society.
So, choked with grief, I pledge my solemn
    word
To lift aloft the banner of MacBird.

ROBERT *lifts aloft a fallen MacBird banner. Robert's*

retainers and MacBird's followers join in bearing the body in a grand procession off-stage. Robert and MacBird banners wave side by side.

Other Black Cat Books

TRAIN TO PAKISTAN. A novel by Kushwant Singh   BA-1   50¢

The passionate love story of a Sikh boy and Muslim girl, set in turbulent India. "A brew of brimstone, blood and nitric acid served piping hot."—*American Scholar*

CAIN'S BOOK. A novel by Alexander Trocchi   BA-2   50¢

"The genuine article on a dope addict's life," wrote the *N. Y. Herald Tribune.* "Just slightly less graphic than Henry Miller," added the *Library Journal.* A candid, ruthlessly honest portrayal of the tortured half-world of drugs and addicts.

JAZZ: ITS EVOLUTION AND ESSENCE

by André Hodeir   BB-3   60¢

Undoubtedly the best and most perceptive book on jazz ever written. "The most penetrating book of its kind."—*New Yorker*

THE FOLKLORE OF SEX by Albert Ellis   BC-4   75¢

An irreverent, revealing dissection of American sexual habits, including extramarital relations, petting, perversions, etc. "Ranks among the important contributions to life and love in the U.S.A."—*American Journal of Psychotherapy*

ON LOVE AND SEXUALITY by Dr. Edrita Fried   BC-5   75¢

A modern, frank approach to sexual apathy, frigidity, boredom, homosexuality, clinging, masturbation, promiscuity, and other problems of self-adjustment.

MUST YOU CONFORM? by Robert Lindner   BB-6   95¢

A challenge to America, and to the demon of conformity, by the brilliant psychoanalyst Robert Lindner, author of *The Fifty-Minute Hour* and *Rebel Without a Cause.*

DRUGS AND THE MIND by Robert S. de Ropp   BC-7   95¢

Whether you smoke, drink, take tranquilizers or have ever been tempted by any of the pills or drugs offered as a short cut to happiness, this book will delight and fascinate you.

RED STAR OVER CHINA by Edgar Snow   BD-8   95¢

The classic, first-hand account of the early years of Chinese Communism, describing the rulers of present-day China, how they took over, etc. Indispensable for an understanding of China today.

LADY CHATTERLEY'S LOVER.

A novel by D. H. Lawrence   BC-9   75¢

Available to American readers after 31 years of suppression. "Ulysses apart, this is the most notorious novel of the 20th Century, prosecuted from Poland to Japan...."—*New Republic*

TROPIC OF CANCER. A novel by Henry Miller   BD-10   95¢
The complete, unexpurgated Grove Press edition. "For me *Tropic of Cancer* stands beside Moby Dick. . . . American literature today begins and ends with the meaning of what Miller has done."—Lawrence Durrell

MAN AGAINST AGING by Robert S. de Ropp   BC-11   75¢
The fascinating story of man's efforts to understand aging and to prolong life and vitality, complete with the most recent scientific information, brilliantly written in clear, non-technical style.

ALCOHOL by Berton Roueché   BA-12   50¢
A famed medical reporter presents the whole history of fermented and distilled beverages. "A 100-proof volume filled with fact and lore. . . . You will enjoy reading it, with or without a drink."—*Los Angeles Times*.

MASOCHISM IN SEX AND SOCIETY
                                    by Theodor Reik   BD-13   95¢
The most frequent and significant of all perversions—man as a pain-seeking animal—is discussed in this extremely readable and enlightening book. "Reik is undoubtedly the best living writer about psychoanalysis. . . ."—*N. Y. Times Book Review*

UNDERSTANDING YOUR CHILD
                                    by Dr. Edith Buxbaum   BA-14   50¢
For all parents: an indispensable guidebook in the elements of child psychology. "The book is simply written and yet no compromise is made on the solidity of scientific observation. It can be put in the hands of mothers at all levels of education and sociological background."—*Parents' Magazine*

THE MIND OF THE MURDERER
                                    by Dr. M. Guttmacher   BB-16   60¢
Drawn from three decades of courtroom experience, this is a comprehensive description of the genus "murderer." "Capsule stories of murder in the raw that pale much comparable fiction."
—*The Saturday Review*

THE INSULTED AND INJURED
                                    A novel by Fyodor Dostoevsky   BC-18   75¢
A major novel by the great Russian storyteller, in which selfless love is pitted against licentious evil.

THE INTELLIGENT HEART:
The Life of D. H. Lawrence by Harry T. Moore   BD-19   95¢
The full, frank story of the volcanic life and loves of the man who wrote *Lady Chatterley's Lover*. "This life of Lawrence is the fullest and most authoritative to date."—*Chicago Tribune*.

SEXUAL ABERRATIONS, Vol. I

by Wilhelm Stekel, M.D.   BC-64 $1.25

A documented exploration of such fascinating topics as the cult of the harem, fetishism and incest, homosexuality, transvestitism, the Satanic Bible, etc.

SEXUAL ABERRATIONS, Vol. II

by Wilhelm Stekel, M.D.   BC-65   95¢

A comprehensive exploration of the sexual distortions known as fetishism, including several that have rarely been documented. Topics include: onanism, impotence, sadism, masochism, etc.

AN INTRODUCTION TO ZEN BUDDHISM

by D. T. Suzuki   BC-66   95¢

The basic text for the general reader interested in understanding Zen. "We cannot be sufficiently grateful to the author."—C. J. Jung

THE EVOLUTION OF PHYSICAL SCIENCE

by Cecil J. Schneer   BC-67 $1.95

A clarification of fundamental ideas in physics, chemistry, astronomy, geology, and mathematics from earliest times to the present.

COUNTERFEIT-SEX by Edmund Bergler, M.D.   BC-68 $1.75

A revised and enlarged second edition of the best-seller work on homosexuality, impotence, and frigidity. "Enlightening and valuable."—*Psychiatric Quarterly*

TWO NOVELS BY ALAIN ROBBE-GRILLET:

Jealousy & In the Labyrinth   BC-69 $1.65

"*Jealousy* is a technical masterpiece, impeccably contrived."—*New York Times*. "*In the Labyrinth* is a great work of literature."—*France Observateur*. Includes analytical essays and a bibliography.

THE CONFIDENCE MAN by Herman Melville

BC-70   95¢

New low-priced edition of Melville's classic novel. "A companion volume to Gulliver's Travels."—Lewis Mumford

PECULIARITIES OF BEHAVIOR, Vol. I

by Wilhelm Stekel, M.D.   BC-71 $1.75

The first study to examine in detail impulsive acts such as the wandering mania, narcotomania, and dipsomania. Includes 50 case histories.

PECULIARITIES OF BEHAVIOR, Vol. II

by Wilhelm Stekel, M.D.   BC-72 $1.75

A pioneering study of the instinct and emotions, particularly of sex. Kleptomania, gambling, pyromania, and allied impulses are thoroughly scrutinized, with the significance of many acts revealed.

SADISM AND MASOCHISM, Vol. II
by Wilhelm Stekel, M.D.   BC-86   95¢
This second volume contains many detailed case histories and covers a range of topics, from cannibalism to self-mutilation.

FEMALE SEXUALITY by Marie Bonaparte   BC-87   95¢
A new low price for this bestselling work on the erotic function in woman, from earliest manifestations to adult behavior.

THE VISIONS OF SIMONE MACHARD
by Bertolt Brecht   BC-88 $1.25
One of Brecht's most tender and moving plays, published here for the first time in an English translation. An original paperback, translated and with preface by Carl R. Mueller.

FRIGIDITY IN WOMAN, Vol. II
by Wilhelm Stekel, M.D.   BC-96   95¢
"A cornerstone in the development of knowledge concerning the psychological factors involved in sexuality."—*Psychiatric Quarterly*.

THE WORLD OF SEX by Henry Miller   BC-97   75¢
This remarkable book—Henry Miller's speculations on sex—treats its subject with the candor which readers have come to associate with all of Miller's writings. It attacks the obsessive American preoccupation with acceptable snide smut, in favor of an open reverence for the sex life.

QUIET DAYS IN CLICHY by Henry Miller   BC-98   75¢
The evocation of Paris, that "lamp lit for lovers in the wood of the world," is gentle, serene, and loving. The work is a beautiful introduction to Miller's other writings.

SEXUS by Henry Miller   BC-99 $1.25
Sexus is the first novel in a trilogy called *The Rosy Crucifixion*, consisting of, in order, *Sexus*, *Plexus*, and *Nexus*. "Miller has once and for all blasted the very foundations of human hypocrisy—moral, social and political."—*The Nation*.

PLEXUS by Henry Miller   BC-100 $1.25
Plexus is the second novel in the Miller trilogy, *The Rosy Crucifixion*. "His boldness of approach and intense curiosity concerning man and nature are unequalled in the prose literature of our times."—Citation of the American Institute of Arts and Letters.

NEXUS by Henry Miller   BC-101   95¢
Nexus is the third novel in the Miller trilogy, *The Rosy Crucifixion*. ". . . what makes Miller distinctive among modern writers is his ability to combine, without confusion, the aesthetic and prophetic functions."—Sir Herbert Read.